MW01118589

Church Planting

by

Rev. Dr. Daniel L. Brown

*To my friend Rev.Dr. Simpkins, Moderator
thank you for your support and
friendship.*

Pastor Daniel Brown

May 2013

RED LEAD PRESS
PITTSBURGH, PENNSYLVANIA 15222

The contents of this work including, but not limited to, the accuracy of events, people, and places depicted; opinions expressed; permission to use previously published materials included; and any advice given or actions advocated are solely the responsibility of the author, who assumes all liability for said work and indemnifies the publisher against any claims stemming from publication of the work.

All Rights Reserved
Copyright © 2013 by Rev. Dr. Daniel L. Brown

No part of this book may be reproduced or transmitted, downloaded, distributed, reverse engineered, or stored in or introduced into any information storage and retrieval system, in any form or by any means, including photocopying and recording, whether electronic or mechanical, now known or hereinafter invented without permission in writing from the publisher.

Red Lead Press
701 Smithfield Street
Pittsburgh, PA 15222
Visit our website at *www.redleadbooks.com*

ISBN: 978-1-4349-6811-1
eISBN: 978-1-4349-2789-2

Table of Content

INTRODUCTION

This writing is an introduction to Church Planting. Church Planting is an awesome task and one that should not be entered into without a close relationship and walk with Almighty God and a Spirit filled commitment to the task at hand through the guidance of the Holy Spirit.

It is important to remember that the real church is the people of God. Therefore, one must think of this task as an additional calling to provide a place for God's people to continue in His Word and in His Service. Thus, there must be disciples/followers that are committed to your Calling and Leadership. Whether it be two or three God will be in the midst and He will provide the increase.

The following is a Step by Step "Walk of Faith" in Church Planting. For your encouragement, I have included a brief synopsis of my personal story as an example of what is to come in following God's calling and guidance of the Holy Spirit as one becomes anointed for church planting.

A PERSONAL REVELATION FROM GOD

A Personal Revelation from God

First Agape Baptist Community of Faith was birthed out of a desire to fulfill my commitment to preach the gospel of Jesus Christ; to provide a peaceful place of worship for God's people; and the ability to service the needs of the surrounding community. God gave me a teaching ministry and a strong desire to grow in the teachings of Christ; and to further realize my calling by Christ to Ministry and the personal growth and development of God's people.

The Church was flourishing and the enrollment and attendance was systematically growing. Teaching and training was in place and, as always in congregations, there was a core group of individuals who were supportive and dedicated to the ministry. However, the big picture of "all is well" did not exist. Unfortunately, the missing link was cooperation and support. What emerged was a lack of cooperation from a spiritually unfulfilled leadership.

Thus, the impetus that fostered this spirited adventure was the persistent lack of cooperation of the leadership and the continuous blocking of pastoral direction, God's vision, and programming projections.

All attempts to resolve the persistent division between the leadership and the pastor was to no avail. Church meetings became more difficult as Christian values rapidly deteriorated and the negative attitude of the leadership prevailed.

I feared for the individuals who were of Christ and the possible damage the situation could inflict upon their spiritual growth. As pastor, I began to realize that a decision was necessary, and one that would result in less destruction to God's people. It was, therefore, important for me to decide whether to remain in the continuously deteriorating situation or to tender my resignation from what had become a volatile position based on the inability of these individuals to compromise and/or yield to any means of a logical solution.

Upon seeking direction through much prayer and conversations with family and friends, a final church meeting left me in anguish. The Lord began to speak to my spirit. I prepared myself for a night of rest, but later discovered that God had a different plan. I felt His presence all around me. He began to speak to me about the direction and decision associated with His plan for my life. He guided me to scripture about the difficulty Jesus had in His Ministry when He was at home and could not heal because of the people's unbelief. This is Jesus who always heals! However, Jesus decided to leave home and take His Ministry to another location. It was very clear that God was releasing me from this assignment. My "season" was over and it was now the beginning of a new season and a new assignment. These spirit filled moments with God was full of His revelation and direction and the ultimate decision I was to make. I was unable to sleep because God's visitation lasted all night.

I received authorization to begin a new ministry. God gave detailed directions for ministries rather than the usual title of boards. The finance of the church was to be administered by a Financial Budget ministry with weekly meetings; Church meetings will be Church Conferences; and there would finally be a community outreach ministry. God continued by naming the outreach ministry, Wholistic Family Agape Ministries Institute and the development of a Teenage Pregnancy Prevention program and HIV/AIDS initiative.

By the time the sun came up, I realized that I had not slept, but had received God's direction all night. The amazing thing about the whole situation, however, was that I felt as fresh as if I had a full night of sleep.

God's power charged me physically, mentally and spiritually. The experience of that night was unmatched by any event in my lifetime. My fate was sealed and my task was at hand. I accepted the plan and immediately began working toward fulfillment. I thank and praise almighty God for that special night of His anointing and vision.

LETTER OF RESIGNATION

4

Rev. Dr. Daniel L. Brown
3111 South 15th Street
Arlington, VA 22204

September 25, 1999

Dear Members:

God has been so good to us individually and collectively. I have been blessed to have served as your Pastor for over thirteen years. I have enjoyed being a part of your family; marriages; baby blessings; ups and downs; trials and tribulations; graduations; retirements; and other special events.

We all know that life is dynamic, moving and seldom static; but quite frankly, I find the present situation extremely unsettling.

I have, along with my loved ones and friends, determined that it is time to launch out into the deep and plant a new church – a Community of Faith. I did not arrive at this decision without consulting with and listening to God. The past months have been quite trying, as it is evident that division has crept into the church family. It is obvious that from some quarters, there is a lack of an appreciation of the direction that God is leading our ministry.

While the ministry God has given me points toward evangelism, outreach and expanded ministry, there is a dissent cry of "we don't want to grow, expand or participate. We desire to remain the same, keep our money for our building, and definitely remain homogenous."

One of the most disconcerting things about our congregation is that we will not confront wrongness. We allow friendship and kinship to silence us when controversy emerges in our church meetings and in important situations.

My dear members, it has become impossible to minister at this Church as God is directing me. The trustees' leadership and the majority of trustees have consciously disagreed with the pastor's vision and direction. There has emerged a schism on the Deacon Board that has strained relationships and pastoral direction. When there are open divisions in leadership, it correspondingly affects the congregation.

As a result, untruths have been circulated and distortions of pastoral views and direction have been projected. My family has been slandered and abused. I have tried as Pastor to be loving and forgiving, even to the point of taking abuse. Even when I offered an apology to the church seeking cohesiveness and togetherness, it fell on deaf ears.

Therefore, after much prayer, meditation and listening to our Lord and Savior Jesus Christ, I deem it necessary to remove myself to ensure that Christ's mandate of my witnessing for Him can be achieved in an atmosphere of harmony and in love.

Renelda and I, along with our family, leave you in Agape love and with peace.

My new ministry will remain in Alexandria and God has already given the name for the church, "First Agape Baptist Community of Faith." Our first service will be held Sunday, October 3, 1999, 12:00 p.m. at the Durant Recreation Center, 1605 Cameron Street, Alexandria, Virginia.

God bless you and yours,

Rev. Dr. Daniel L. Brown
Pastor

VISION PLANTING

Vision Planting

My next move was to share the vision and gather those individuals to share the task of implementing God's Plan. Thus, I made several telephone calls to bring a positive group of God's people together to receive the Plan.

The following represents a meeting between those individuals who were selected as the administrative team to share in the planning process. This particular group of individuals was selected to represent a cross-section of individuals to represent the various segments of the population of a church congregation.

THE VISION

Church planting is an awesome, rewarding, fulfilling experience. It is extremely challenging and one must have a calling from God to ensure success. Yes, you must have God's blessing and you must have support from those who are able to catch the vision and have a passion for the ministry.

There are many factors that encroach upon the positive formation in the Church planting process. Let me share some of these factors that impacted my ministry.

The **First Factor is one of being sure that God has spoken to you** and that He clearly commanded the planting process. If you hear another voice other than the Lords the awesomeness of the tremendous event will create failure rather than success.

The **Second Factor is the priority of faith**. Without faith it is impossible to please God. We must have faith that what God spoke concerning the church planting will take form even when sight, voice and spiritual insight suggest otherwise. Remember you are building that which does not exist. Faith is imperative. Hallelujah!

The **Third Factor is the importance of a Spiritual Support System**. You must be firmly, rooted and grounded in your faith. You must know who you are in Christ and understand your relationship to your significant other. If you have a spouse, your spouse must be completely on board with the mission and vision. Additionally, you need a "spiritual encourager" who will stick through thick and thin situations and times.

The **Fourth Factor is to surround yourself with a core group**. This group will be the beginning leadership model and catalyst for propelling, and maintaining the God given mission and vision of the planted church.

The **Fifth Factor is the formation of the formal organization of the church.** One must know the projected vision; short range goals; ministry purpose; ministry priorities; potential ministry leaders/catalyst; and "start up worship service." This must not be in one's head but recorded in writing.

The **Sixth Factor is securing a church office that is large enough for meetings**; conferences; and ministry group meetings (such as choirs; ushers; missionaries, Deacons, Deaconess, Trustees, and other selected ministry groups).

The church office can and must serve as the "church home" if the church worship center is in a school house, recreation facility or some other building. This must be viewed as a priority and will serve as a beginning and temporary base of operations.

The **Seventh Factor is to advertise to the greatest extent possible**. We immediately placed an article in the local newspaper concerning our church, the vision, the time and place of worship. Having a positive public relationship is a necessary ingredient for establishing a solid community relations and presence which will inevitably propel you toward a peaceful start-up existence.

The **Eighth Factor is to develop and establish seed funding** as a means of securing a financial base to serve all aspects of the ministry that most assuredly will demand finance. If a stable financial base is not in place; then a budget will not be in place and it will be impossible to plan appropriately.

The **Ninth Factor is to plan interesting, spiritual and fun filled community/fellowship events** for the first year and each succeeding year. Observe Thanksgiving, Christmas, Easter Season, New Year's Eve, Mother's Day, Father's Day, Youth Sunday, Scholarship/Education Sunday, Graduation Celebration, and Vacation Bible School.

The **Tenth Factor is to stress "Finding Them and Keeping Them."** Place great emphasis on Discipleship rather than membership. Stress commitment and the expectation of Discipleship rather than volunteerism of membership.

The **Eleventh Factor is to closely observe the planting process of the designated Church.** The church should go through four designations: **Missions** Church; **Essential** Church; Church **Completion**; and finally **Church Recognition** which is performed by a body of selected Baptist fellowship groups. The selected groups may be from the Northern Virginia Baptist Association; the Baptist General Convention of Virginia; the National Baptist Convention Incorporated; Progressive National Baptist Convention; the American Baptist Convention and/or others.

As Baptist, the Church begins/starts as a mission group. This mission group works toward becoming an Essential, Complete and Recognized Church. It is not advantageous to short cut this process as this may cause potential problems later in the life of and recognition of the Church.

The Mission Church is in its formative state. The mission Church remains so until it starts to take form and begins to work through the Essential elements of the formal organization such as; Church officers, Church discipline, Church Worship and Church Ministries.

ADMINISTRATIVE PLANNING MEETING

FIRST AGAPE BAPTIST COMMUNITY OF FAITH
Administrative Planning Meeting Minutes
August 31, 1999

Rev. Dr. Daniel L. Brown officiated the meeting of August 31, 1999.

A group of ten individuals volunteered to attend the meeting and were selected as the Official Administrative Planning Team for Church Planting. The meeting was called to order by Rev. Dr. Daniel L. Brown with the reading of scripture (Psalm 18:1-26) followed by prayer.

Dr. Brown's opening statement consisted of a brief presentation on the purpose of the meeting which was the appointment of an administrative team to engage in dialogue regarding his attempt to develop and design a smooth transition into church planting. He expressed the importance of the administrative team to consist of a cross representation of church leadership; Deacons, Deaconess; Trustees, Missionaries and individuals involved in church administration.

Dr. Brown verbalized a detailed message emphasizing his decision to tender his resignation as Pastor of his present church; as well as his God given vision to plant/establish a new Church.

II. DECISION

Rev. Dr. Daniel L. Brown stated that as he engaged in prayer/conversation with God it was apparent that he would establish a new church. The church was to minister to God's people in two areas: First there would be the establishment of a household of faith designed to carry out the preaching of God's Word to the saved and unsaved under the name of "First Agape Baptist Community of Faith." Secondly, there would be the establishment of an outreach ministry designed to service the needs of the local community as, the "Wholistic Family Agape Ministries Institute." Dr. Brown announced that he applied and received a tax exempt 501(c)(3) status in the Commonwealth of Virginia which would enable a smooth transition into his anticipated outreach efforts.

III. A NEW BEGINNING/VISION

A. Statement of Purpose:

We hereby establish/set aside and dedicate the concept of a "wholistic family" ministry. This wholistic concept will involve a wholistic approach in serving individuals through mind, body and spirit. Therefore, our charge will be to minister to those who are in need physically, emotionally and spiritually. The focus of this ministry will be about people. It is and will be our charge to evangelize. It is and will be our charge to establish a place for

12

God's people to edify and buildup his name so that the name of Jesus may coalesce for kingdom building.

Dr. Brown informed the group that it was important to feel that you are capable of performing in the same capacity that you see others and that you have the ability to do it well. He emphasized that he personally never thought of himself as being incapable of achieving any goal he felt worthy of achieving. However, he never envisioned planting a church, but the events and circumstances led him in this direction. He expressed that he was pleased with the number of individuals, who were the leaders of their particular ministry, who made the decision to follow him. This was encouragement for him and confirmation that nothing is impossible to achieve. Dr. Brown emphasized that, throughout the coming weeks, there would be a dependence on God through much prayer to accomplish the task at hand. "The thief cometh not, but for to steal, and to kill, and to destroy: I am come that they might have life, and that they might have it more abundantly." (John 10:10)

B.   Areas of Ministry:

1.   **Worship**: Dr. Brown emphasized the importance of worship and that church leadership must be aware of a Board's intent. Boards have the propensity to take on a life of their own, and can lose sight of their original purpose and spirituality. Historically, the church has two biblically ordained officers/leaders; the Pastor and Deacons. He noted that when others feel they have authority, confusion develops, and a multi-headed vision does not work and will lead to multiple problems. He emphasized that the new church's leadership structure will be ordained deacons and ministers. Trustees will exist to enhance the work of the deacons but are not ordained. The new church will replace the concept of boards with Ministry. (Example: Deacon Ministry, Trustee Ministry and Christian Education Ministry). The word BOARD will not be used. The Church will be governed exclusively by God's Covenant, and will not entertain the idea of a secular document known as a Constitution. It will be the responsibility of all Deacons to be cognizant of all individuals within the Household of Faith, to ensure that negativity and bad attitudes will be cause for intervention by Deacons to circumvent any unacceptable behavior in the house. We must guard against a reluctance to confront individuals on issues, whether family or friends. It is Dr. Brown's hope to plant the type of church that models what a church is to be, according to God's plan and purpose.

Dr. Brown expressed the importance of spirituality in worship. The church must participate in teaching and training for the purpose of spiritual growth; and our focus must be the praise and adoration of God. He envisioned a falling away from the type of worship that became a part of the former church congregation. He indicated he would be working with the ministers and deacons in this area and adjustments will occur in the program format of worship service.

2. **Training**: All training will come under the Christian Education Ministry. We will continue our efforts with three Deacons presently in training. It is our expectation that others will come. The trustee in training at the former site will complete his training in the new church. The current Director of Christian Education will remain in that position in the new site.

3. **Evangelism**: Dr. Brown expressed that evangelism was an area of extreme importance to him. Thus, he will be working with the ministers to move this ministry in a positive direction. Others who are interested in evangelism will be encouraged to participate.

4. **Outreach Ministries**: Dr. Brown stated that it is presently not known whether the Welfare to Work funding will be achieved. However, we will continue, through the Wholistic Family Agape Ministries Institute, to coordinate and implement additional planning. In the interim, we will continue to conduct Bible study at the Ladrey Senior Building, and we will be able to continue our present Prison Ministry, to include aftercare. The Share food ministry will be temporarily housed at the Charles Houston Recreation Center. Additional ministries will be projected as resources become available.

C. Place-Site-Timing:

Dr. Brown informed the group that on the 3rd Sunday in September he will announce a Special Joint Board meeting at the former church, to be held on the following Tuesday. He will submit his resignation to the Board at that time and make an announcement to the church the following (4th) Sunday. He will have a letter prepared for the congregation to receive the Monday after his announcement to the church.

The temporary site of the new church, "First Agape Baptist Community of Faith" will be at the Durant Recreation Center, 1605 Cameron Street, Alexandria, VA. The main room of the facility has been reserved from 12 – 2 p.m. In addition, we will have two classrooms to house Church School classes. One room will accommodate twenty-six (26) people, and the other twenty (20). The Center will cost Two Hundred Sixty Dollars ($260.00) per week for the use of the main auditorium for worship, and Fifty Dollars ($50.00) per week for classrooms. Space was requested/reserved for Friday evenings to accommodate Bible Study and Prayer Service. Dr. Brown anticipated confirmation of the reservation and will submit the initial Eighty Dollar ($80.00) deposit.

Dr. Brown expressed his personal preference of having our first service on a "First Sunday" to enable us to give honor to God through the incorporation of Communion on the day of our first service, as well as to consecrate the first Sunday as our day to commemorate this service. The immediate essentials necessary for the first service was stated to be: Communion set, collection plates, Bibles and Hymnals. The estimated cost for these items was said to be Two Thousand Five Hundred Dollars ($2,500.00).

Individual Assignments by Ministry:

A potential list was developed to represent individuals who would unite with the Church. The list was reviewed in terms of ministry leadership and/or interest to ensure that major leaders would be in place.

Mission (Church Status) Set Aside by Council Affiliations – City, District, State, National

A brief synopsis of the procedures necessary for church planting was presented. Dr. Brown informed the group that we first become a mission. The next step is to be recognized by the Council to become recognized as a complete/full Baptist church in association with the Baptist denomination.

He further stated that the church will participate and be affiliated with the Baptist Associations; i.e., the Northern Virginia Baptist Association, Baptist General Convention of Virginia and the National Baptist Convention.

The need to establish a bank account was stated and a discussion ensued regarding the appropriate procedure for establishing an account. A former trustee volunteered to secure an "employer identification number" (EIN) and ensured the group that he would take care of all of the preliminary work for establishing the account; and anticipated completion within two weeks. It was suggested and agreed that office space be obtained to appropriately coordinate a home base for all ministry efforts. An individual was selected to accomplish this task.

The question was asked whether to prepare a form letter to the former church to expedite the immediate change in membership for those individuals joining "First Agape Baptist Community of Faith." The decision was to do so and a letter was drafted for that purpose.

D. Financial Structure

Dr. Brown stated that as pastor of the new Church the financial structure of the church will be Trustee Ministry; Treasurer Ministry; Clerk's Office; and Secretarial /Administrative staff.

Individuals asked about funding and the source of income for the first few months. After a brief discussion, it was unanimously agreed that this could not be determined. Dr. Brown stressed the importance of maintaining our focus; working together and to move toward becoming a tithing church. He warned individuals to put aside the negative experiences of the past to ensure that none would be carried into our new setting.

Dr. Brown was informed that some individuals had set aside funds/tithes to be used as seed money for the new church ministry. Thus, a September

12th date was scheduled for individuals to have an opportunity to present the funds/tithes.

The group engaged in additional dialogue regarding budget issues. The question was raised as to the type of financial package envisioned for the pastor in terms of salary since the records currently showed, as of the first Sunday in October, the only one present in the meeting that would be without a salary was the Pastor.

Dr. Brown addressed the group on the importance for the new church, "First Agape Baptist Community of Faith," to develop an attitude of "taking care of their pastor." He stated that this attitude did not exist within the previous church. A positive attitude toward leadership should come before anything we decided to do, to include a building. If the leadership is nurtured, the ministries will flourish. He was in agreement to have the group develop and submit a salary package for the pastor to be placed in the budget.

As the pastor, Dr. Brown expressed that it is his expectation to be involved and/or included in regular budget discussions and the financial matters of the new church. He expressed the need for this Community of Faith to avoid the idea of excluding/blocking the pastor from the financial matters of the church. He emphasized that Pastoral leadership includes the responsibility to develop the church in all areas, including finance.

Additional budget items were discussed and the need for transportation became another essential concern (van ministry). Thus, the search would begin for a 15 passenger van to purchase. Weekly rentals were estimated to cost approximately Seventy-five Dollars ($75) per week. (Potential members offered their personal van for church use.) In the interim personal vans would be used and magnetic signs would be purchased to identify them for church use.

Dr. Brown created/developed a worship service for seniors wherein he traveled to a local senior hi-rise building to allow the residents who were sick and shut-in to hear the Word of God. The group discussed the need to continue this Worship Service. However, it would be necessary to check the availability since we are not aware of whether the former church might decide to continue, as well. Thus, we will consider the first Sunday in November, upon availability.

Two individuals spoke of the need for the church to have a logo and volunteered to participate in its design.

Since the new church will hold worship service at a recreation center, the possibility of a potential problem regarding staffing and facility use for holiday services (i.e., Christmas and Thanksgiving) was questioned. Dr. Brown discussed briefly and individuals volunteered to work on a resolution regarding potential problems.

A special word of thanks was extended to everyone who participated in this the first meeting for the "planting" of First Agape Baptist Community of Faith. The meeting was adjourned with closing prayer by Rev. Dr. Daniel L. Brown, pastor.

SECOND ADMINISTRATIVE

PLANNING MEETING

FIRST AGAPE BAPTIST COMMUNITY OF FAITH
Administrative Planning
Second Meeting - September 22, 1999
Agenda

I. Brochures
    - Ministry
    - Welcome Packet
    - Public Relations

II. Budget

III. Order of Service
    - Altar
    - Setup
    - Choir
    - Bulletins
    - Agape Greeters
    - Recording

IV. Past/Present/Future Attitudes

V. Computer Needs

VI. Office Space/P. O. Box

VII. Ministries
    - Training (Deacons/Deaconess/Trustees)

VIII. Finance/Offering Envelopes, etc.
    - Bank Account

FIRST AGAPE BAPTIST COMMUNITY OF FAITH
Administrative Planning Meeting

September 22, 1999 - Minutes

The Church Planting Meeting of September 22, 1999 was held at the home of Rev. Dr. Daniel L. Brown and Mrs. Renelda E. Brown at 7:30 p.m.

Rev. Dr. Daniel L. Brown, pastor officiated the meeting and opened with the reading of scripture (Psalm 1) followed by prayer. Dr. Brown informed the group that the first meeting of First Agape Church was a good one. He presented brief highlights from the minutes of the August 31, 1999 meeting.

The Agenda was followed with Dr. Brown announcing to the group that a letter from him will be mailed on Saturday, September 25, 1999 to members of the former church announcing his decision to resign. The letter would be delivered by U.S. Mail and received by the congregation on Monday, September 27, 1999. The announcement to the Church will be made on Sunday, September 26.

A joint board meeting was held at the church on Tuesday, September 21, in a very subdued atmosphere. One of the members asked a question that made others appear to, in that particular moment, realize that the pastor and others leaving did not set well with the church. A statement was made that without his presence the finances (tithes and offerings) would not be as they were.

Dr. Brown stated that he was pleased with the meeting and hoped that the subdued atmosphere was not, "the calm before the storm." He further stated that it is over! History....

Dr. Brown informed the group of their newness and ability to move forward to establish the kind of church and ministry God desires. A building cannot take precedent over ministries. The main focus of the Church is the praise and worship of Almighty God. The second is to have a service oriented ministry. Walls have contained us. We do not have walls now. It is his expectation that God will prosper, bless and grow us. Constraints have been lifted. If we sit down, plan and come together we will be able to do it!

Dr. Brown presented a list of the possible ministries for the new church. He expressed having six deacons; a Church Clerk; Assistant Clerk; Treasurer and an Assistant Treasurer; six trustees; a Director of Christian Education; Church School Superintendent; two assistant superintendents; Altar Guild; Deaconess Ministry; Stewardship Ministry; Musicians; Choirs; Usher; Missionaries; Media Ministry; and a secretarial staff as his core leadership group. In addition, he announced the addition of the following ministries:

A Drama Ministry; Agape Bible Institute; Beautification Ministry; Scholarship Ministry; Nursery Ministry; Spiritual Ambassadors; Senior Ministry; Bible Study-Senior Building; Women's Ministry; Men's

20

Fellowship: Save the Seed (Male Youth); Newspaper Staff; Youth Bible Ministry; Hospitality Ministry; Nursing Unit; Youth Council; Prison Ministry; Youth Choir: Boy Scouts; Girl Scouts; Junior Ushers; Praise Dancers; Senior Ushers; Youth Ministry; Van Ministry; and a Couples and Singles Ministry.

The meeting continued with a brief discussion regarding letters for members to change their membership. It was decided that letters would be sent from the Church Clerk for those individuals in leadership positions; Deacons, Deacon Chair, and Trustee Chair. Letters would be prepared for members who wish to withdraw their membership. All letters will be available after the September 26, 1999 service.

A welcome packet was developed and discussed at the meeting. Everyone received a copy of the packet and after a brief discussion the group approved the packet as a visitor's and new member's handout.

Office Space: The next discussion was focused on obtaining office space. Dr. Brown will be meeting to negotiate a facility on Mt. Vernon Avenue this week. The estimated price range will be from $1,500 to $1,900 per month. The space is large enough for meetings, office space and ministry meetings. There are a few parking spaces located at the back of the building. A donation of items, such as a desk and chairs were offered and accepted. Dr. Brown will purchase approximately 40 chairs as soon as we obtain the space.

Post Office Box: The question was raised as to whether we will need a post office box. The group voted to obtain a post office box.

Computer: Two individuals volunteered to work on the purchase of a computer system that is viable and inexpensive. Dr. Brown instructed them to make an immediate purchase within the next few days.

Public Relations: Dr. Brown indicated the need for a public relations team which will prove to be extremely important. First will be the necessity to publicize our new church; while the other would be to effectuate timely communications to counter any negatives targeted at our new setting. Current methods of public relations are: Agape Greeters; media and personal encounters (doing what we say we will do). Dr. Brown noted to the group that approximately Thirty-two Dollars ($32) per week was spent on communication letters.

Service Cancellation: Dr. Brown selected a volunteer to work with him on ways to spread the message regarding service cancellation due to inclement weather.

Sunday Program/Bulletin: A Sunday bulletin was necessary for the worship service. Dr. Brown and two volunteers will finalize this project. A decision regarding the design and other particulars will be necessary prior to publication.

Membership: Members are responsible, First to engage in worship. Second, is the expectation to join at least one ministry, (this is a minimal requirement). In actuality, two to three are equivalent to reasonable service.

Finance: Two individuals volunteered to initiate the development of offering envelopes and to create a checking account for the Church.

Projected Budget: A projected budget document was circulated and a discussion ensued, however, the group decided not to move forward in that more time was needed for further study.

It was noted that individuals submitted personal contributions, as start-up funds, to create a Bank Account (all names and amounts were recorded).

The meeting was adjourned at 11:30 p.m. with closing prayer by Dr. Brown.

THE MISSION

THE MISSION

There must be a First/Initial Call Meeting after the decision to formulate/plant a church. Since the church is the people of God it is important that you are in the process of establishing a meeting place for those who are committed to the task/mission at hand.

Numbers at this point are not important. What is important is that God is in the plan and He has anointed you to provide a vision/place whereby His people will receive spiritual nurturing to grow in grace and in the knowledge of Jesus Christ our Lord, Master and Savior.

Planting requires one to move out of their comfort zone. You must test the waters by getting out of the boat and, through faith, walk on water with Jesus.

In addition to pastoral leadership, the church will need other leaders. This leadership group should consist of the selection of Deacons; Deaconess; Church Clerk; Trustees; Choir; Music Director; Musicians; Ushers, etc.

Select a group of disciples to provide additional leadership and insight. Come to the meeting with a plan along with a list of those items necessary for a smooth transition. This includes the selection of a group of Officers to assist in performing the necessary beginning tasks.

First Agape Baptist Community of Faith

Welcome

To The

"THE GENESIS OF NEW BIRTH"

Dedicated to the pure worship of God
The awareness of service to the Lord our God
To evangelize and wholistically minister to the poor

For Today Only, Oct. 3, 1999

Welcome to First Agape Baptist Community of Faith. If you are thinking of uniting with this Church and you are currently a member of an existing church, please complete this form in advance, and hand it to one of the Deacons when instructed to do so by the Pastor. We also invite you to attend our New Member's Reception immediately following this Worship Service.

First Agape Baptist Community of Faith

Ministry Office
2619 Mount Vernon Avenue
Alexandria, Virginia 22301
(703)519-9100

Rev. Dr. Daniel L. Brown,
Pastor
Temporary Location
Durant Recreation Center
1605 Cameron Street
Alexandria, VA 22314

October 7, 1999

To Our New Members:

Welcome to First Agape Baptist Community of Faith!

We are so pleased that you have decided to become a part of this First Agape Baptist Community of Faith.

We recognize God has been good to us, and we desire to see you become an active, service oriented member of this Church. Please come prepared to allow God to use you for His glory. We have enclosed your initial tithing envelopes, and will send additional more systematized envelopes in the near future. Please make sure you record your full name on each envelope to assist us in keeping accurate records for you.

We have also enclosed our Membership Information Form. We understand that many of you were not able to complete your form when you joined First Agape at the October 3rd service, and would appreciate your completing this form and submit to the Church Clerk, Pat Tyler; or the Assistant Church Clerk, Kimm Sydnor.

If you have any questions about First Agape's ministries, or would like to talk to me personally at any time, I can be reached at (703)519-9100.

Yours in Christ,

Rev. Dr. Daniel L. Brown
Pastor

First Agape Baptist Community of Faith
P. O. Box 0000, Arlington, VA 22222 (703)000-0000

NEW MEMBER INFORMATION VERIFICATION

First Name	Middle Initial	Last Name

Address Apt.	No City/	State	Zip

Home Phone	Work Phone	Cell No.

Names/Ages of Minor Children (Please Indicate Member/Nonmember):

_____

_____

_____

_____

New Members Class Attendance ___ (1) ___ (2) ___ (3) ___ (4) ___ (5)

Date Joined_____ Baptism Date_____ R/H Fellowship Date:_____

OPTIONAL INFORMATION:

Occupation_____

Special Skills:_____

Special Talents_____

MINISTRY/AUXILIARY/ORGANIZATION INTEREST

_____

_____

OTHER RELEVANT INFORMATION

_____

_____

_____

First Agape Baptist Community of Faith

Ministry Office	Rev. Dr. Daniel L. Brown,
2619 Mount Vernon Avenue	Pastor
Alexandria, Virginia 22301	Temporary Location
(703)519-9100	Durant Recreation Center
	1605 Cameron Street
	Alexandria, VA 22314

October 25, 1999

To Our First Agape Community of Faith:

> *"But ye are a chosen generation, a royal priesthood, an holy nation, a peculiar people; that ye should shew forth the praises of him who had called you out of darkness into his marvelous light." I Peter 2:9*

We thank God for the opportunity to be able to be part of the planting of a new church. It is an exciting and exhilarating experience that demands the very best of all of us. Therefore, we are praying for the health and well-being of each member specifically, and their extended families.

God has truly smiled on us for these four weeks, and everyone seems to be happy in our present setting. We realize that we do not have a permanent church house, but the important thing is that we are the church building. Therefore, we must remember that together we make up the First Agape Community of Faith. On the 3rd Sunday in October, it was suggested that every member of the congregation take on a new middle name of "Agape." We look forward to continuing growth in Jesus Christ as our Lord, Master and Savior.

"Now he that ministereth seed to the sower both minister bread for your food and multiply your seed sown, and increase the fruits of your righteousness; being encircled in everything to all bountifulness, which causeth through us thanksgiving to God." 2 Cor 9:10-11.

We have enclosed tithing envelopes for your use through the end of the year. **"So let each one give as he purposes in his heart, not grudgingly or of necessity; for God loves a cheerful giver."**
2 Corinthians 9:7

Yours in Christ,

Rev. Dr. Daniel L. Brown
Pastor

28

First Agape Baptist Community of Faith
Ministry Office
2619 Mount Vernon Avenue
Alexandria, Virginia 22301
(703)519-9100

December 27, 1999

Letter to Former Church

Attn: Chairman, Board of Deacons and Church Clerk

This communication is forwarded according to traditional Baptist Church polity. The following named brothers and sisters in Christ, all former members of the previous Church congregation, have expressed their determination to terminate membership with your Church and have entered into a Covenant relationship with First Agape Baptist Community of Faith.

Therefore, you are respectfully requested to remove the said individuals from your membership records upon receipt of this notice.

Further, for the accuracy and authenticity of our records, please acknowledge receipt of this communication.

Sincerely,

_____
Acting Church Clerk

_____
Acting Chairman, Deacon Ministry

CHURCH ESSENTIAL

Church Essential

The second meeting of church planting should move the planning emphasis to the focus of church essential. This focus will particularly involve those things that are necessary for the church to function.

One must move from the initial planning state to a reality state. The plan is now ready for implementation. It is time to identify and organize your first day of Sunday worship service.

Your beginning faith must explode with a greater knowledge of the power of Almighty God and the fact that He propels man's impossibilities into reality. One must use their creative energy to visualize and create a list of essentials to complete the plan.

Viewing a service we see preaching from a pulpit; voices propel from a PA system; we hear the music from musicians and singing from a choir. We see/hear a diaconate prayer from a deacon; we hear announcements from a church clerk; we see the tithes and offerings filling the collection plates; we see ushers in their places; we see trustees position for action and we conclude this vision with a word from God...."the people will come" and when they do they will be anxious to receive a program/bulletin of the service.

Further, if your first service is scheduled to occur on the first Sunday of the month, which in many church settings is significant as Communion Sunday, your list must include the essentials for communion.

However, your decision and plan may have been to have communion on the first day of worship to honor and remember God for what He continues to do in the lives of His people, even if your first day of worship is not scheduled on the First Sunday.

First Agape Baptist Community of Faith

Ministry Office	Rev. Dr. Daniel L. Brown, Pastor
2619 Mount Vernon Avenue	Temporary Location
Alexandria, Virginia 22301	Durant Recreation Center
(703)519-9100	1605 Cameron Street
	Alexandria, VA 22314

November 15, 1999

To: The Northern Virginia Baptist Association

As many of you have heard, I recently made the decision to resign as Pastor of my previous Church. We all know that life is dynamic, moving and seldom static. But quite frankly, I found the situation at this church Extremely spiritually unsettling, and determined that it was time to launch out into the deep and plant a new church – a Community of Faith. Today, I am pleased to announce to you the beginning of my new ministry – **The First Agape Baptist Community of Faith.**

— The Genesis of New Birth –
Dedicated to the pure worship of God
To the awareness of service to the Lord our God
to evangelize and wholistically minister to the poor.

My new ministry will remain in Alexandria, with offices at: 2619 Mt. Vernon Avenue, Alexandria, VA 22301, Phone 703-519-9100; Fax: 703-519-9510.

Our worship services will be temporarily housed at the Durant Recreation Center, 1604 Cameron Street, Alexandria, Virginia, and will begin at 12:00 noon. In addition, we have developed an outreach ministry, Wholistic Family Agape Ministries Institute, and will begin community efforts in the very near future.

I look forward to continuing to work with the Northern Virginia Baptist Association, moving forward in our efforts for Kingdom building.

If we at First Agape Baptist Community of Faith can help you in any way, please let us know.

Yours in Christ,

Rev. Dr. Daniel L. Brown

32

First Agape Baptist Community of Faith

Ministry Office2619 Mount
Vernon Avenue
Alexandria, Virginia 22301
(703)519-9100

Rev. Dr. Daniel L. Brown,
Pastor
Temporary Location
Durant Recreation Center
1605 Cameron Street
Alexandria, VA 22314

November 17, 1999

Rev. Dr. Kenny Smith, Moderator
Northern Virginia Baptist Association, Inc.
6703 Hanson Lane
Mount Air, Virginia 22079

Dear Moderator Smith:

It is the intent of the newly planted/formed First Agape Baptist Community of Faith to be recognized by the Northern Virginia Baptist Association, Inc., as soon as possible.

God moved in my life in an unusual and unexpected way which culminated in the vision and planting of the idea of a church and the subsequent realization of the same.

As Pastor of the former Church in Alexandria, VA, for thirteen plus years, I felt it necessary to tender my resignation to the Church Joint Board on September 21, 1999, and my formal resignation to the Church Body on Sunday, September 26, 1999.

God blessed my ministry for the thirteen plus years at that Church and I am eternally grateful. God has also blessed my ministry to continue without any break in service, as we were able to continue with the first worship service on October 3, 1999 at the Durant Recreation Center in Alexandria, VA. Ninety-four persons came to be a part of the ministry on that day. Presently through the grace of God, we now have 142 members.

The following Ministries are intact and functioning: Deacon, Trustee, Deaconess, Missionary, Christian Education, Church School, Youth and Young Adult, Usher, Adult, Music, Mass Choir, Young Adult, Agape Angels, Agape Greeters, Praise Dance, Treasurer, Assistant Treasurer,

Volunteer Secretary, and a Budget/Finance Committee (Deaconess in Training).

The Church has leased 1900 square feet of office space located at 2619 Mt. Vernon Avenue, Alexandria and will be worshipping across the street in the Mt. Vernon Elementary School beginning in January 2000. God has blessed our Ministry in every way and I am thankful, I ask your continued prayers as we move forward in Kingdom Building together.

Please inform me and the membership as to the procedures for our recognition beyond God's recognition and sanction to be set aside as an organized Baptist Church. The Officers and membership desire to be set aside at the earliest convenient date.

Yours In Christ,

Rev. Dr. Daniel L. Brown
Pastor

cc: Dr. Carson Wise
New Church Coordinator

P.S.   At the November 9, 1999, Fall Session, First Agape Baptist Community of Faith officially joined the Baptist General Convention of Virginia.

First Agape Baptist Community of Faith

Ministry Office
2619 Mount Vernon Avenue
Alexandria, Virginia 22301
(703)519-9100

Rev. Dr. Daniel L. Brown,
Pastor
Temporary Location
Durant Recreation Center
1605 Cameron Street
Alexandria, VA 22314

December 18, 1999

To Our First Agape Baptist Community of Faith:

We are now in our third month as First Agape Baptist Community of Faith, and we thank God for the opportunity to continue to be able to fulfill His vision. The planting of a new church is both exciting and exhilarating and demands the very best from all of us. We pray each day for continued health and well being of our members and their families.

We have enclosed tithing envelopes for the first quarter of 2000. "So let each one give as he purposes in his heart, not grudgingly or of necessity; for God loves a cheerful giver." (2 Corinthians 9:7)

God is truly smiling upon us. We are now blessed to be able to move into a setting that will be more conducive to our growing needs.

- Beginning New Years Eve, December 31, 1999, we will have our worship services at Mt. Vernon Elementary School, 2601 Commonwealth Avenue, Alexandria, VA. The New Years Eve Family Night and Watch-night Service will be from 9:00 p.m. to 12:00 a.m. Please see our bulletin for further details on this night of Christian celebration.

- Our first Sunday service at the new site will be January 2, 2000, with Church School beginning at 9:45 a.m., and the worship service beginning at 11:00 a.m.

- Please mark your calendar for our Stewardship Day, Sunday, January 9th beginning with Rev. Archie Richmond as guest speaker at our 11:00 a.m. worship service, followed by a fellowship meal and ending with an interactive workshop session.

We look forward to our continuing growth in Jesus Christ as our Lord, Master and Savior. I am praying God's continued blessings upon you during this special holiday season.

And thou, child, shalt be called the prophet of the Highest: for thou shalt go before the face of the Lord to prepare his ways; To give knowledge of salvation unto his people by the remission of their sins, Through the tender mercy of our God; whereby the DAYSPRING FROM ON HIGH hath visited us, To give light to them that sit in darkness and in the shadow of death, to guide our feet into the way of peace. (Luke 1:76-78)

Yours in Christ,

Rev. Dr. Daniel L. Brown
Pastor

CHURCH COMPLETE

The First Church Meeting

"Church Complete"

The first meeting is attended by those individuals who have joined/united with this body of believers in Christ Jesus and is an essential step toward church complete.

Representation from the governing body of the local Baptist Association must be present to perform the task of "Setting Aside" the Church as a Church Complete.

Church complete is a church prepared and ready to teach and preach the Gospel of Jesus Christ to the saved and unsaved.

To God Be The Glory!

Church Essential becomes Church Complete when it is recognized by a formal gathering of the local and/or district Baptist Association and receives the blessing of this formal gathering through the presentation of the following resolutions:

1. A Resolution on how the church will be consecrated;

2. A Resolution on acceptance of the Articles of Faith;

3. A Resolution on Scriptural Guidance;

4. A Resolution on Parliamentary Procedures;

5. A Prayer of Blessing for the Church;

6. An Offertory for Missions;

7. A Formal Election of the Pastor must be achieved for Church Complete;

8. All Officers and Ministry Leaders are formally presented (voted upon), a Motion received and seconded; and a majority vote achieved;

9. The Meeting is formally adjourned; and

10. A Formal Record of the proceeding is accomplished.

After Church Complete the process goes to the Baptist Association for review, evaluation and acceptance (that is if the church wishes to complete this phase).

I hesitate to state that the church can choose to be independent as some churches have become. However, I do not recommend that the church become an island as such. This suggests a desire to be self sufficient by keeping funds in house; and a lack of a desire for fellowship and instruction through an organizational body of Baptist churches. It is without question that we must draw strength from each other and maintain a fellowship community among believers.

First Agape Baptist Community of Faith

Ministry Office	Rev. Dr. Daniel L. Brown, Pastor
2619 Mount Vernon Avenue	Temporary Location
Alexandria, Virginia 22301	Mt. Vernon Elementary School
(703)519-9100	2601 Commonwealth Avenue
	Alexandria, VA 22301

CHURCH MEETING MINUTES
February 6, 2000

The First official church meeting of the First Agape Baptist Community of Faith was held on Sunday, February 6, 2000, beginning at 1:00 p.m.

Moderator: Rev. Dr. Lloyd O. Roberts, Pastor
              Ebenezer Baptist Church, Alexandria, VA

The meeting was called to order by Rev. Dr. Lloyd O. Roberts, Pastor of Ebenezer Baptist Church; at which time the group was led into a devotional period by Minister Joanne Bates. Rev. Dr. Daniel L. Brown, Founder and Acting Pastor of First Agape Baptist Community of Faith, opened the meeting with an explanation of the purpose of the meeting which was to set apart First Agape as a bona fide Missionary Baptist Church. Since its inception four months ago First Agape was recognized first as a "mission," next as "church essential" and after this church meeting will be categorized as "church complete." Dr. Brown recommended that Rev. Lloyd Roberts be selected as Moderator, to preside over this meeting. A motion was made and unanimously carried that Rev. Lloyd O. Roberts preside over the meeting.

Rev. Lloyd Roberts began by requesting a formal record of the said meeting be recorded in the form of minutes. A motion was made and carried that the administrative secretary record the minutes.

The first order of business was an explanation by Rev. Roberts to address the First Agape congregation regarding the rules and procedures for the meeting. He asked that only those individuals who joined First Agape by letter or Baptism make formal motions and seconds to motions. Dr. Brown indicated that twenty-five (25) individuals joined First Agape through Christian experience (or by letter); and fourteen (14) joined by Baptism. He also recognized one individual who joined by letter from a local church (Alfred Street Baptist Church), however, the letter was mailed but not received prior to the meeting.

40

Rev. Roberts ruled that this individual qualified to participate in the meeting process, as well as the other thirty-nine members stated by Dr. Brown.

Rev. Roberts presented the following resolutions to the First Agape membership:

A Resolution on how First Agape will be constituted:
- We do hereby, Resolve and state that we believe by the Holy Spirit, and relying on the blessing of God, we do, by this act, constitute ourselves as a Church of Jesus Christ to perform His service, and to be governed by His Will, as revealed in the New Testament, and to this end, we do hereby adopt and agree to the following covenant and "articles of faith."

Rev. Roberts asked for the congregation's response to the Resolution. The congregation responded unanimously to accept the Resolution.

A Resolution to Accept the Articles of Faith:
- Rev. Roberts presented, reviewed and interpreted the Articles of Faith.
  Rev. Roberts asked for the congregation's response to the Resolution. The congregation responded unanimously to accept the Resolution.

A Resolution on scriptural guidance:
- Rev. Roberts stated that the Holy Bible will be the scriptural guide.
  Rev. Roberts asked for the congregation's response to the Resolution. The congregation responded unanimously to accept the Resolution.

A Resolution on parliamentary procedures:
- A Resolution was presented to follow the Hiscox Manual as the guide to parliamentary procedures.
  The First Agape membership unanimously agreed to abide by the Hiscox Manual as their guide to parliamentary procedures.

Rev. Roberts offered a prayer asking God's blessings on First Agape and its membership. Following the prayer, he announced that First Agape Baptist Community of Faith, was no longer a "mission" but was now duly organized as a Missionary Baptist Church. The question was then asked of the membership; "who would serve as the pastor of the First Agape Baptist Community of Faith." The membership response was: A motion was made and second to elect/accept Rev. Dr. Daniel L. Brown as pastor of the First Agape Baptist Community of Faith. The motion was carried by a unanimous vote of the membership.

Rev. Roberts guided the congregation through the customary procedure of an offering for missions. Dr. Brown requested the First Agape Missionary Ministry to use the offering to uplift one of its missions. It was decided that the offering would be sent to the Virginia Baptist Children's Home.

Rev. Roberts then recognized the Deacons and Deaconess from his church. (Ebenezer Baptist Church), who came to witness the meeting to formally organize the new church.

Rev. Dr. Daniel L. Brown and the membership of First Agape offered a vote of thanks to Rev. Roberts for presiding over the meeting. Dr. Brown at this time, formally requested the installation of all Officers and Ministry Leaders for First Agape. The officers/leaders were presented and a motion was made and unanimously carried to accept the individuals as the Year 2000 Leadership for First Agape Baptist Community of Faith. The newly elected pastor, Rev. Dr. Daniel L. Brown, adjourned the meeting with prayer.

FIRST AGAPE BAPTIST COMMUNITY OF FAITH
STRUCTURE OF LEADERSHIP

The structure of Leadership begins with the Pastor. The pastor's support and next in command/leadership comes from the Deacon Ministry and is followed by the Ministerial Staff.

The successive line up will be the Trustee Ministry, Treasurer, Budget and Finance, Administration Ministry, Music Ministry and the Christian Education Ministry. These ministries are supported by the Presidents' Council which represents the presidents and chairs of all ministries. Thus, the leadership structure ends with the Church Ministries/Congregants.

NEW DISCIPLE PROCESS FLOW

This process represents the flow of new disciples as they enter the church in search of a Church Home and are classified as a "visitor." The ownership of the visitor is the Evangelism Ministry, Spiritual Ambassadors and the Minister of Evangelism. The personal contact for the individual is the person responsible for the invite. The individual upon entering the church will become the focus of the Ushers and the Agape Greeters and will receive a brochure narrating all church ministries.

At the end of Worship Service, the pastor immediately focuses on greeting each visitor. This greeting and welcome is followed by a personal letter from the pastor in recognition of the visit. The Agape Greeters will maintain contact with each visitor to ensure their return. Visitor returns and joins with the Body of Christ.

Membership: The Membership process begins with the Deacon's verification of readiness for membership and whether by Christian Experience or Baptism. Individual's personal information is recorded (both hard copy and electronically) by the Clerk and disseminated to Deacons and Spiritual Ambassadors. A notification letter regarding change in membership will be mailed to former church.

Church Orientation: The new disciple is required to attend four sessions in either the adult or youth "New Disciple's Class." Upon completion a date is set for baptism; and upon baptism the Right Hand of Fellowship and participation in their first Communion will occur on the first Sunday of the month following baptism. New disciple will receive church tithing/donation envelopes.

Disciple will receive teaching to understand "Spiritual Gifts" and upon completion will select a ministry of service. Disciple is encouraged to attend Church School and Bible Study, as well as to participate in all activities and programs of the Church.

TITHING & OFFERING PROCESS FLOW

The Church functions off of the tithes and offerings of the membership. The process flow of these transactions begins with the member presenting tithes/offering. At the time of the presentation the owner is the ushers and the ushers raise it toward heaven to receive a blessing. At the end of worship the trustee ministry claims the finances and retires to the Trustee Office to count and record the amount collected.

All envelopes containing tithes and offerings are opened, checked for accuracy and recorded. All cash funds are separated and added accordingly. The recordkeeping process is categorized by Church School; Missions; Building Fund; Ministry Gifts/Seed planting, etc. The treasurer claims the funds and preparation is made for deposit. A copy of the amount of funds deposited is forwarded to the Pastor, Trustee Chair, Budget & Finance Committee and Clerk.

The tithing/offering envelopes are forwarded to the Clerk. The Clerk records the funds in each member's financial record and each member is given a copy of his/her total funds allocated for the year at the end of each year.

Additional financial records are recorded and maintained by Budget and Finance in terms of processing the income and expenses. All expenditures and income of the church comes under the scrutiny of the Pastor and Budget and Finance Committee which comprises of a cross section of the leadership of the church. These individuals meet on a weekly basis. All financial records must coincide with the records of the Treasurer and the Clerk in order to maintain balanced records.

WITHDRAWAL OF FUNDS

All activities of the Church must be approved by the Pastor. Ministry Leaders must submit a pre-approved form for requesting funds for church related activities to Budget and Finance. Budget and Finance must determine when the finances are needed and whether there is sufficient funds to process the request. Providing the account is validated by the Treasurer the check is processed and all necessary signatures affixed and the request is submitted to the requestor.

RECLAMATION PROCESS FLOW

The Spiritual Ambassadors are essential to maintaining contact with the membership. A complete an accurate record of the membership is maintained both in hard copy and electronically.

The Church Clerk maintains a record of each disciple's financial records while the Spiritual Ambassador's focus is on attendance. Telephone calls, cards and letters have been established as the process of communication to maintain consistent contact with all disciples. All disciples who are missing four consecutive Sundays are referred to the Pastor and Deacons. A letter is sent to establish a reason for inactivity and to reclaim the disciple to regular attendance.

CHRISTIAN EDUCATION MINISTRY

The Pastor is the Ex Officio Officer of the Christian Education Ministry based on his position as pastor of the Church. The Director of Christian Education is under the direct supervision of the Pastor in carrying out the functions of this Ministry.

The hierarchy of leadership within the Baptist Church is the Pastor and Deacons. In addition and next in line is the church's Ministerial Staff. Only the pastor is directly over the Deacon Ministry and this is by design according to scripture.

The Ministry of Christian Education is responsible for Teaching and Training for all ministries within the church. Thus, all ministries are directly influenced by the Christian Education Ministry in the following ways:

- Church School
- Bible Study
- Workshops
- Conferences
- Programs and Activities
- Educational Opportunities
- Seminars

MUSIC MINISTRY

The Pastor is the presiding leader of the church and all ministries fall under his leadership and supervision. As always, in the Baptist Church, the Deacons follow him in terms of the hierarchy of leadership. The ministerial staff is under the pastor but does not relate or involve the Deacons.

The Music Ministry is directly under the supervision of the pastor. The Music Ministry must develop its own leadership within the music department to insure the ability to positively process the function of this ministry within the church. There should be a Minister liaison person, and a president. Each choir must have a leader and all leaders of each choir are under the responsibility and supervision of the Choir President and the Minister of Music.

The Pastor

Rev. Dr. Daniel L. Brown of Arlington, Virginia has been a pastor in the City of Alexandria, VA for twenty-six years. Dr. Brown has pinned two books. His first book is the result of an outreach program he developed to provide assistance to victims of HIV/AIDS; alcohol and substance abuse; the prevention of teen pregnancy; improving parenting skills among young adults and low self-esteem within both groups.

Dr. Brown has a passion for people and his acceptance of the "call" to ministry provided the opportunity to make a difference in the lives of individuals in need. His second book is designed to provide an opportunity for one to find moments of peace and a spiritual oneness of calm and serenity. It is meant to be an escape from the difficulties of life enabling the ability to connect with God. His third book is on "Church Planting," which provides a detail synopsis of how one plants a church. Dr. Brown planted, First Agape Baptist Community of Faith, October 3, 1999.

Dr. Brown received his associate degree in Education from Norfolk State University; a B.S., in Education, from Virginia State University; MA in Guidance from George Washington University; Ph.D., in Education, from Walden University; Master of Divinity from the School of Theology, Virginia Union University; further study at the University of Virginia, and Appalachian State University in Leadership; and two interns at the University of Maryland.

Dr. Brown retired from the Arlington County Public School System after thirty-four years of service. He held the following positions: Fifth and Sixth Grade Teacher; Child Development Consultant; Elementary School Principal; Director of Human Relations; Director of School Community Relations; Adult Night School Principal; and Adjunct Professor, University of Virginia.

He is a licensed professional counselor for the State of Virginia and the American Psychotherapy Association; awarded the designation of Diplomate for APA; and a Board Certified Professional Christian Counselor of the International Board of Christian Counselors.

First Agape Baptist Community of Faith

First Agape Baptist
Community of Faith
Ministry Office
2619 Mount Vernon Avenue
Alexandria, Virginia 22301
(703)519-9100

Rev. Dr. Daniel L. Brown,
Pastor
Temporary Location
Durant Recreation Center
1605 Cameron Street
Alexandria, VA 22314

Date:_____

TO: _____

_____

_____

Thank you so much for your very kind donation.

This is to certify that _____, valued at _____, was donated to and has become the property of First Agape Baptist Community of Faith.

Please let us know if you need any additional information.

_____

Treasurer

_____

Assistant Treasurer

CHURCH ASSOCIATION(S) RECOGNITION

First Agape Baptist Community of Faith

Ministry Office
2619 Mount Vernon Avenue
Alexandria, Virginia 22301
(703)519-9100

Rev. Dr. Daniel L. Brown, Pastor
Temporary Location
Mt. Vernon Elementary School
2601 Commonwealth Avenue
Alexandria, VA 22301

April 3, 2000

Rev. Dr. Carson E. Wise
20 Madison Street, N.W.
Washington, D.C. 20011

Dear Dr. Wise:

It is my understanding that we are to formally apply for official church recognition status with the Northern Virginia Baptist Association. On Sunday, April 2, 2000, we had our Church Recognition Celebration service, at which time we were formally approved by the Council of Pastors from the Northern Virginia Baptist Association.

Therefore, our next step is to come before the Executive Board of the Northern Virginia Baptist Association and assure them that we have completed all four recognition stages, to include mission, essential, complete, and recognized. We intend to be at the Northern Virginia Baptist Association's Executive Board meeting on Saturday, April 8th, to complete the recognition process.

Further, we at First Agape Baptist Community of Faith are satisfied that the Lord has blessed us in this church planting endeavor.

Yours in Christ,

Rev. Dr. Daniel L. Brown
Pastor

OUTREACH MINISTRY

FIRST AGAPE BAPTIST COMMUNITY OF FAITH

- The Genesis of New Birth -
Dedicated to the pure worship of God
To the awareness of service to the Lord our God
And to evangelize and wholistically minister to the poor

Outreach Ministry

WHOLISTIC FAMILY AGAPE MINISTRIES INSTITUTE

Working to overcome family difficulties
Through the spirit of strength,
The spirit of hope,
The spirit of Agape love

Rational/Reason for Ministry

Over the years, as I observed our children in the school system, and as I observed our families within my church setting, it became more and more apparent to me that the deterioration within our communities is the direct result of the even more serious deterioration of the family unit. As a society we have not been able to adequately resolve the very basic issues that contribute to every aspect of difficulty our society continues to experience. Drugs, Violence, Teen Pregnancy, HIV/AIDS, Truancy, Digital Divide, Unemployment, Underemployment are all symptoms of basic issues that we have ignored for too long. Surely there is enough blame to go around for all of us, i.e., schools, churches societies and families.

Also, it became obvious to me that the approaches to resolve these very basic issues are isolated, and at times fragmented have not been very effective. Wholistic Family Agape Ministries Institute was founded to attempt to address difficulties within our society that are a direct result of the breakdown of family unity. WFAMI provides a coordinated effort that speaks to affecting change within the total person and/or persons constituting the family constellation. The sole objective of WFAMI is to foster family unity through wholistic ministry - the training and development of the mind, body and spirit.

As a part of the faith based community, I recognize that there is no adequate forum to provide for the enhancement of human qualities of "wholeness." However, there needs to be established, nurtured and, more importantly, maintained an enhancement for human qualities. As a part of a faith based community, I recognized that a trained mind, without a trained spirit, is a partial human being. While governmental bodies can attempt to legislate education and behavior, they cannot legislate the patience, tolerance, racial understanding, love of self, and acceptance of one another. The faith community understands that education without the development of effective human skills is failure oriented. WFAMI, therefore, offers a plan of total - "wholistic" - educational involvement.

Wholistic Family Agape Ministries Institute

IMPLEMENTATION/STRUCTURE

Ministry cannot be viable without adequate human and financial resources.

This ministry has been blessed to recently receive seed money for the beginning of ministry programming:

HIV/AIDS City Wide Conference - from Center for Disease Control
HIV/AIDS Outreach to Hispanic Community - Coordination with Whitman Walker Clinic
HIV/AIDS Prevention and Awareness Program - HUD

- Teen Pregnancy Prevention Program - Freddie Mac Foundation

WFAMI RELATIONSHIP TO FIRST AGAPE

Churches in general have been defined by their physical identity. When, in fact, a church is truly people. Therefore, it is imperative that we design a contemporary and ever-changing church model from a people posture. It is, therefore, necessary to stop viewing our churches as physical entities, and view them from a multi-ministry-driven organism. We cannot continue to view our HELPING RELATIONSHIP from a medical model of specific driven remediation, but a comprehensive wholistic preventative-driven strategy mission. Our problems have a genesis, and to continue to look at and treat only the resultant is fool-hearted and failure oriented.. To accomplish this effort in the most effective way takes more than a volunteer church ministry. Volunteers, although well meaning, do not provide the structure and continuity necessary to implement a viable program. A church in worship can operate off of PRESENCE, a church in ministry takes supreme effort in service:

Wholistic Family Agape Ministries Institute is designed as an entity COMPLETELY SEPARATE from First Agape Baptist Community of Faith. Funding for WFAMI will be completely separated from First Agape church funds.

- Unlike a "normal" church outreach, WFAMI is a 501(c)(3) organization
- Unlike a "normal" church outreach, WFAMI is a state corporation
- Unlike a "normal" church outreach, WFAMI receives funding from outside foundations/government organizations, private organizations, and individuals (not necessarily members)

TO THE FIRST AGAPE LEADERSHIP:

WHOLISTIC FAMILY AGAPE MINISTRIES
WILL BE NEEDING SERIOUS, COMMITTED HELP
FROM OUR LEADERSHIP
AND OUR CONGREGATION

PLEASE LET US KNOW IF YOU ARE WILLING TO BE A PART OF THIS OUTREACH MINISTRY BY COMPLETING THE PORTION BELOW, AND DESIGNATE YOUR AREA OF INTEREST/EXPERTISE.

TO: WHOLISTIC FAMILY AGAPE MINISTRIES

FROM: _____
          Name   Phone No.

I am interested in assisting with community outreach projects being implemented by Wholistic Family Agape Ministries. I feel I can help most in areas concerning:

- Social Service Assistance
- Counseling
- Administrative
- Finance
- Life Skill Workshop Development
- Mentoring
- Other

CHURCH HISTORY

FIRST AGAPE BAPTIST COMMUNITY OF FAITH CHURCH HISTORY

The Rev. Dr. Daniel L. Brown is the founder and pastor of First Agape Baptist Community of Faith Church of Alexandria, Virginia. God gave him the vision to plant a new church upon giving his resignation as pastor for thirteen years at Third Baptist Church of Alexandria. Dr. Brown is a former educator in the Arlington County School System. He is a native of Virginia, and attended Norfolk and Virginia State University. He holds a Masters Degree from George Washington University; a Ph.D. from Walden University; a Master of Divinity from Virginia Union School of Theology; two Administrative interns from the University of Maryland; and further work at the University of Virginia and Appalachia State University.

On the first Sunday in October of 1999 the Reverend Dr. Daniel L. Brown came together with approximately ninety-four individuals and the First Agape Baptist Community of Faith Church became a reality. The first service was held in the Durant Recreation Center in the City of Alexandria, Virginia. Dr. Brown preached Gods Word in spirit and in truth and many were added to the membership. As months passed, the Church moved from the Durant Center to the Mount Vernon Elementary School. During this period the Church rented space across from the school and established a church office. The office was used for various church activities, such as meetings; choir rehearsals; and for the pastor's newly developed Wholistic Outreach Ministry to enable him to minister to the community. Another important feature of this office was that the Church now had a facility to store all of the necessities and equipment used to transform the school into a Church.

On April 2, 2000 First Agape was Recognized as a Church by the Moderator of the Northern Virginia Baptist Association, Rev. Dr. Kenny Smith. Many of the officers and Clergy from the Association were present to voice their approval (Rev. John Johnson; Rev. Lloyd O. Roberts; Elder Mick Upshur; Rev. Tom Bailey, Rev. Eugene Johnson and Rev. James Brown, etc.). Dr. Brown was indeed thankful to God and the membership joined him in offering praises to God.

The struggle was not easy but God remained faithful and continued to bless First Agape. Once again, the Pastor, (Rev. Dr. Daniel L. Brown), through divine guidance selected the present church home at 2423 Mount Vernon Avenue, Alexandria, Virginia as the future site for First Agape. The Pastor wanted the Church to move out of the school into a more permanent facility. He encouraged the members to visit the facility he selected. Many took the short walk to the building and in spite of its condition, ("unclean and unfinished with oily residue"), were able to, through spiritual eyes, see this building as the new home of First Agape. Thus, individuals, such as Deacons, Deaconess, Missionaries and laypersons, walked around in a circle inside the building, shouting praises to God. The group in a leap of faith walked around the building, on the outside, seven times while claiming the property as the future site of the First Agape Baptist Community of Faith. God is true to His Word and is faithful. He answered their prayer and on Sunday, February 4, 2001 Church Service was held in the new home. God was given the praise and glory for all that He had done.

This Church was established and dedicated for the work of kingdom building. Dr. Brown established First Agape with over twenty ministries. In faith he looked to God for more leaders and new disciples to do even greater works according to the Word of God. Many who were in leadership sacrificed tithes and time to Gods service under the leadership of Dr. Brown to assist him in his Ministry through obedience to the Holy Spirit.

Dr. Brown knew that a growing Church must have a biblical foundation. A Church School and regular program of Bible study for both Youth and Adults was established. The membership under his leadership grew in the agape love of Christ. Individuals began to love and care about one another. Many made incredible sacrifices of love to help others. They exercised great faith in praying for one another. The motivating power in church growth is prayer. The Church flourished and many of its needs, as well as the needs of the people were met without begging or selling. Dr. Brown established First Agape as a "Tithing Church" based on God's Word. He instructed his members that the most important thing was not the edifice or how well the organizational structure was developed, but how they humbled themselves to the Will of a perfect, all powerful and loving God and by uplifting people and their needs in prayer. Dr. Brown set goals to address the needs of the surrounding community, while at the same time he preached and taught the empowering of the Holy Spirit, whereby each member would desire and obtain spiritual growth. The Pastor's vision was to purchase the present building in early 2003. God enable all of the visions of the leadership of First Agape to bear fruit.

In March of 2003, God enable First Agape to purchase the entire building they called home. The lyrics of the song "Great Is Thy Faithfulness" was felt throughout the house. The Church was truly thankful and prayed for wisdom, knowledge and understanding as they moved forward in kingdom building for their Lord, Master and Savior. Their hope was in God raising new leaders and new disciples for First Agape to do even greater works according to His Word. God has and is continuing to bless this Community of Faith through His Word as delivered by His messenger, Pastor Brown. The members and friends of First Agape leave each service with a cup overflowing with the gospel of Jesus Christ. Again, Pastor's statement "A growing church must have a biblical foundation" is a reality.

Agape is the unconditional love of Jesus Christ. Thus, First Agape was founded on love. This Church exemplifies love and love radiates throughout the First Agape family. The members love and care about one another. Within this House individuals are making incredible sacrifices of love to help others. They are exercising great faith in praying for one another. The motivating power in church growth is love working together with prayer. It continues to be God's people humbling themselves unto a perfect, all powerful and all loving God, while lifting people and their needs in prayer. The Church has individuals who are giving in abundance in tithes and offerings. Talents and gifts are offered up and there is tremendous growth in witnessing for the Lord and individuals desiring to know more and more about Jesus.

A growing church must permeate evangelism from pillar to post. Everything that is said and done must be for the purpose of drawing others to Christ. The major concern must always be people. The Deacons of First Agape are continually supportive of their Pastor and offer many prayers to God for all of First Agape to move toward spiritual growth. The Church needs God's Word to grow spiritually and God has provided an anointed leader to accomplish this task, in the name of Jesus. The vision of the pastor gives a clear understanding of First Agape's purpose. At present, all of First Agape is in an attitude of growing the church. All members are positive about their church life. Thus, all are in the correct state of mind to initiate church growth (positive attitudes). First Agape's Pastor has set goals to address the needs of the surrounding community through a Wholistic Outreach Ministry, while at the same time preaching and teaching the empowering of the Holy Spirit, whereby each member will desire and obtain spiritual growth, and continue to work together with a focus and commitment toward obedience to God's Word as set forth in the "great commission;" "Go ye therefore, and teach all nations, baptizing them in the name of the Father, and of the Son, and of the Holy Ghost:.." (Matthew 28:19). Gospel means "good news," and is the good news of Jesus Christ. To God be the Glory!

Years of preaching and teaching, while ministering to Alexandria's Youth and the HIV-population of the City, has culminated into the celebration of twelve years in God's Service. We have, by the Grace of Almighty God, continued to add to our membership/discipleship; provide spiritual enlightenment and renewal; impacted lives in terms of academic and professional growth and achievement. Blessings have come in all sizes and packages. We have beautiful pews, an organ, chandeliers, stained glass windows and a baptismal pool.

We have been blessed with good friends who have truly blessed us. We have managed to create a positive image within our community and are actively seeking to provide hope to the hopeless; food for the hungry and continue to be creative and inspired by whatever God desires of us. God's Word has many promises that He is ready to give in response to obedience.

Rev. Dr. Daniel L. Brown continues to serve as First Agape's pastor. His preaching and teaching is all inspiring. Individuals within this household of faith have read the entire Bible during the period of October 2008 thru September 2009. Dr. Brown continues to serve and provide leadership to the Baptist General Convention of Virginia; the Northern Virginia Baptist Association; and the National Baptist Convention, U.S.A., Inc. During the year 2012, First Agape became duly aligned with the National Baptist Convention and the Progressive National Baptist Convention. He has been the recipient of many awards and commendations for his outstanding leadership and untiring efforts as he continues in God's Word. Dr. Brown ordained two women ministers and continues to provide training for deacons and trustees.

First Agape has been guided by the Agape Love of Jesus Christ throughout its twelve years of service. Under the leadership of its pastor, this Household of Faith will continue its efforts in welcoming individuals in the House whereby they are provided an opportunity to know Jesus and accept Him as their Lord and Savior. The teaching and training that continues to occur within First Agape is essential to the spiritual growth of the church. The Church is the people of God and God wants His people to grow.

The church has been successful in reaching those in need through the community outreach programming of the Teenage Pregnancy Prevention Program/Teenage Enrichment Program; while servicing the needs of individuals with HIV/AIDS for the past twelve years. The church continues to receive God's favor in its role of ministering to God's people.

Truly the Lord is faithful and full of blessings and for this we are thankful.